van helsing's night off

and

other tales

by

Mahler

ISBN 1-891830-38-4
1. Cartoons / Humor
2. Horror
3. Graphic Novels

Top Shelf Productions
PO Box 1282
Marietta, GA
30061-1282 USA

www.topshelfcomix.com

Published in 2004 by Top Shelf Productions, Inc.
Publishers: Brett Warnock and Chris Staros.

First Printing. Printed in Canada.

van helsing's night off

and other tales

Some of the following stories originally appeared in the French anthology *Lapin*, published by L`ASSOCIATION.

table of contents

the vampire

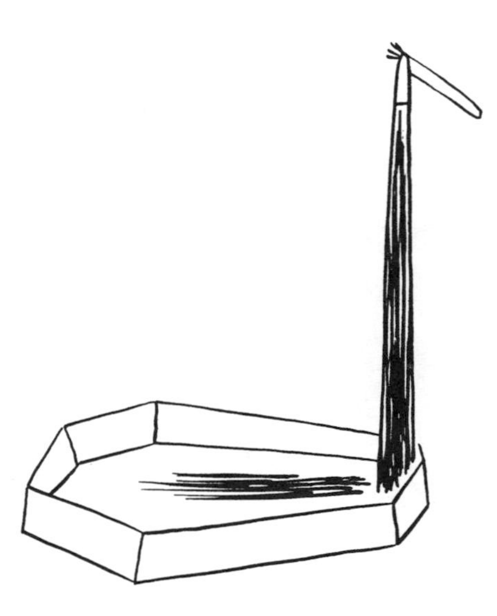

bAR

bAR

MAHLER.

van helsing

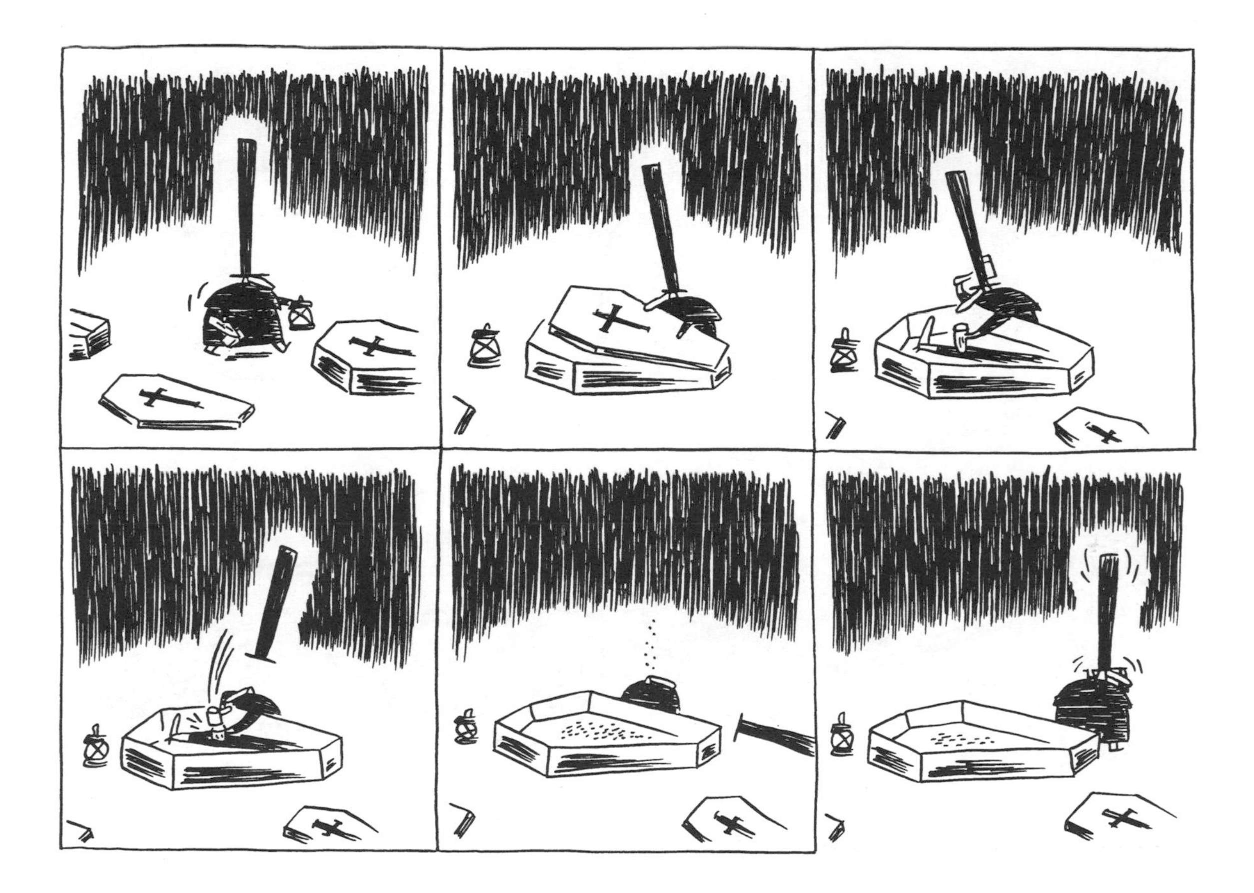

hats
hats
hats

MAHLER

the wolf ma'am

MAHLER

the masked avenger

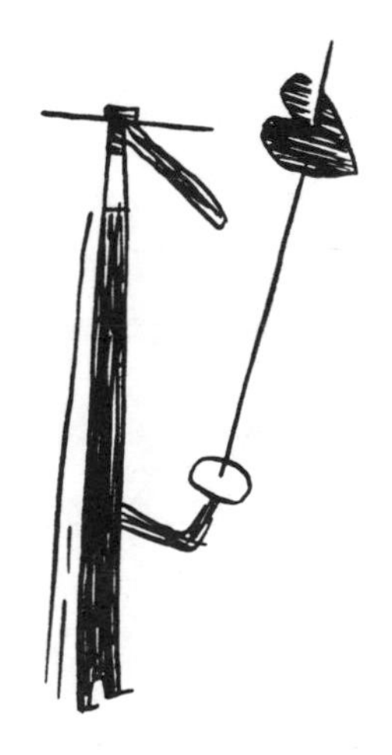

bar
bar
MAHLER

the wolf ma'am II

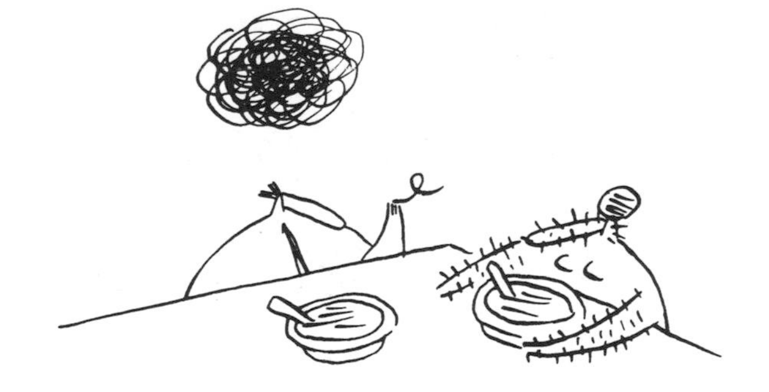

FUCK FEAST
MAHLER

the mummy meets the wolf man

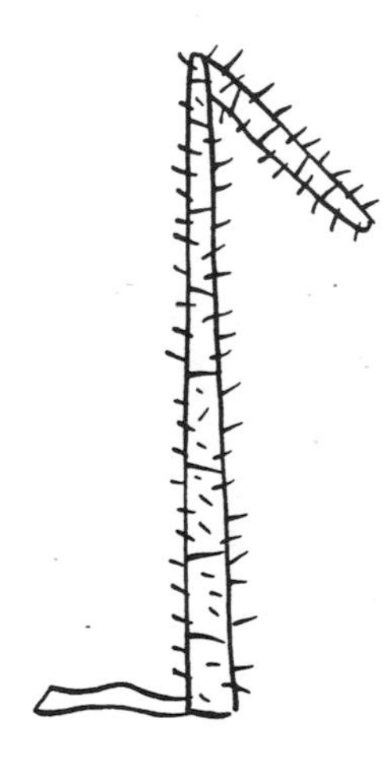

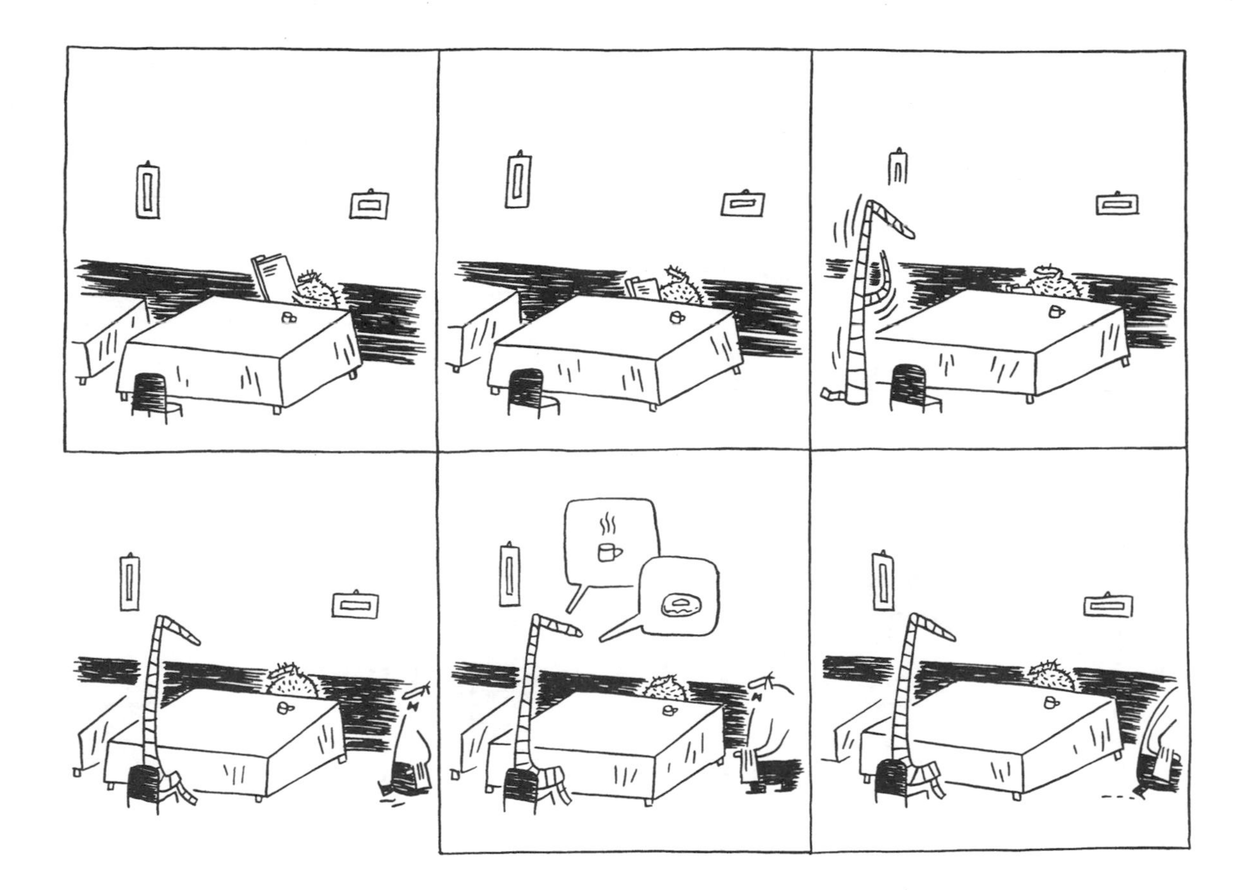

Café

disco
disco
disco
MAHLER

the man with two heads

BAR

MAHLER

the mummy meets frankenstein

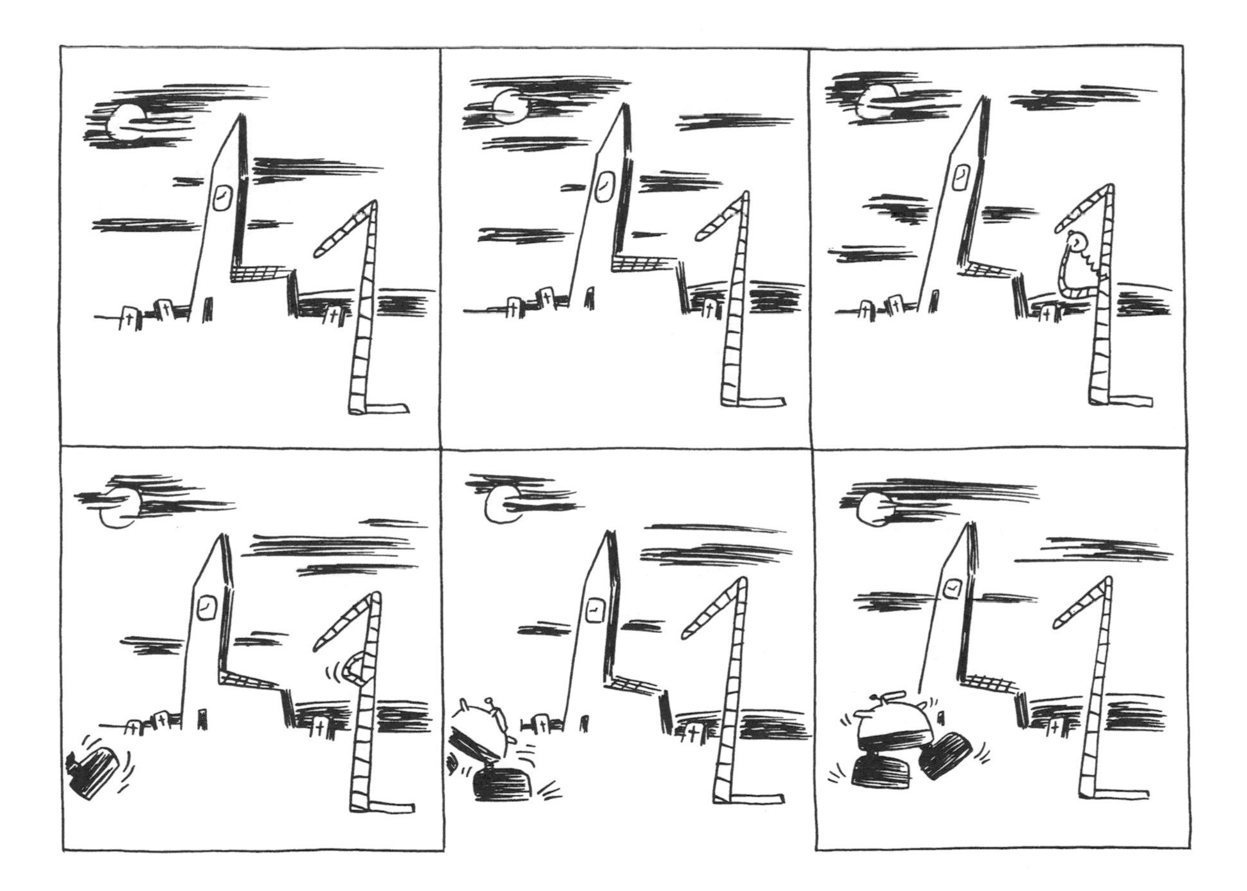

E 1990

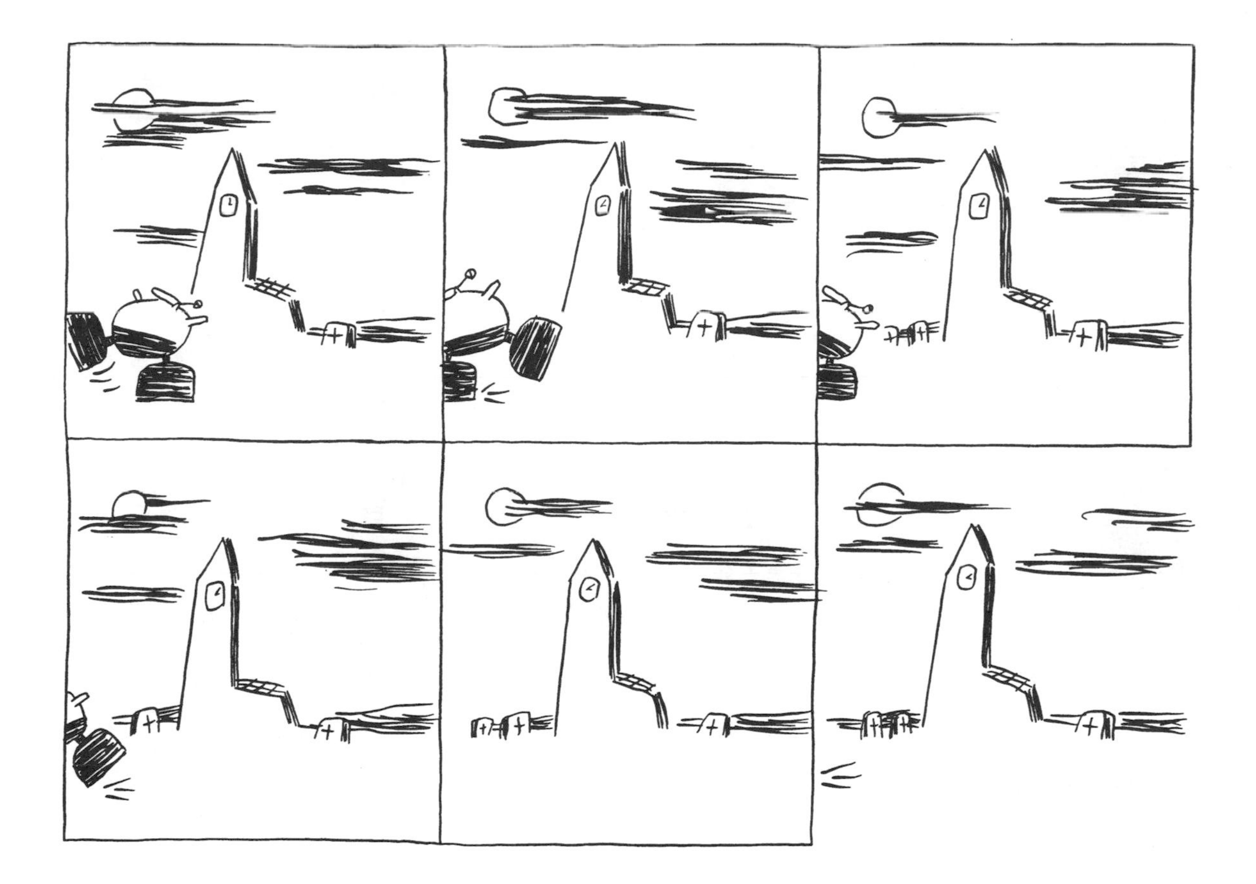

MAHLER

van helsing, ladies man

MAHLER

frankenstein meets the wolf man

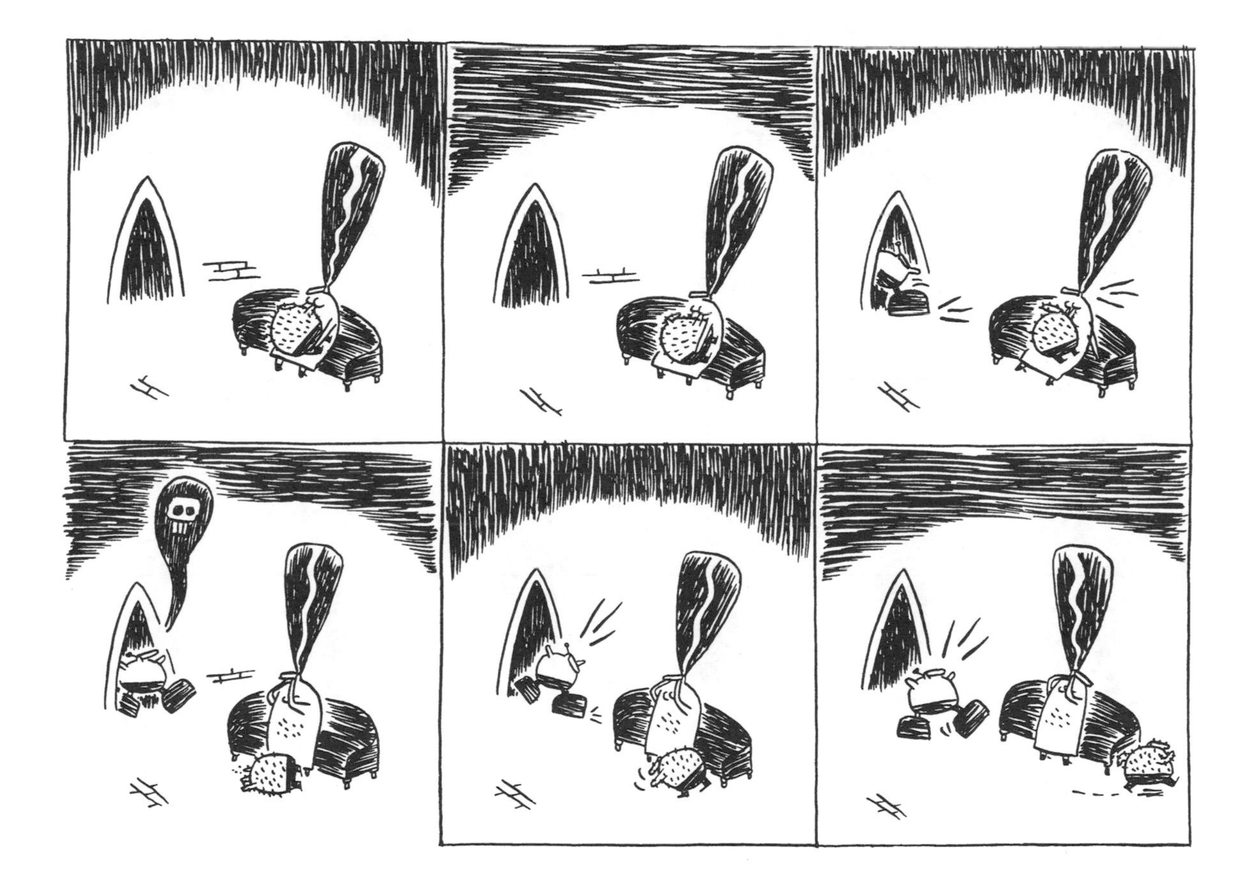

MAHLER

the mad magician

MAHLER

the masked avenger vs. the wolf man

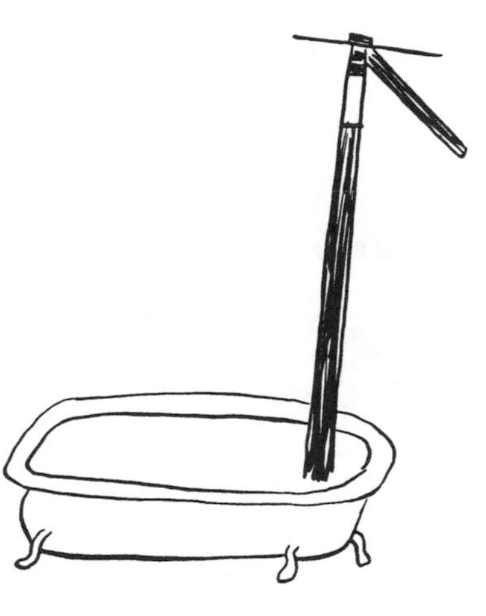

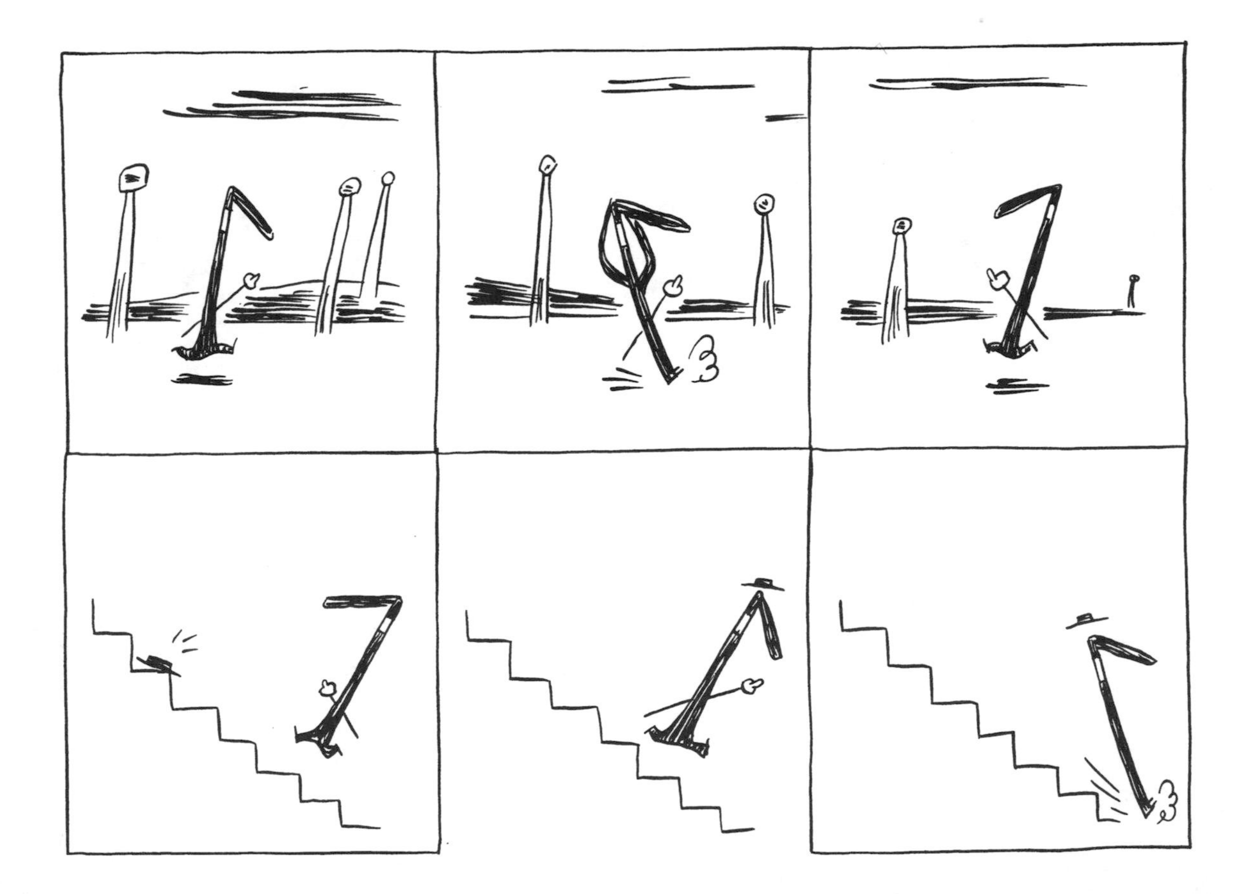

MAHLER

the invisible man

bar

bar
bar
MAHLER

mummy in a white suit

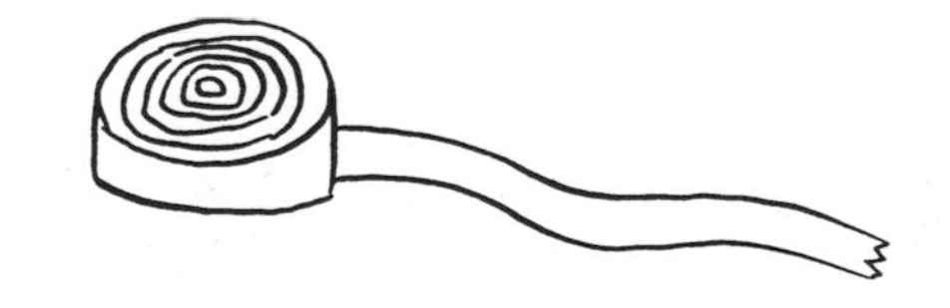

MAHLER

the masked avenger vs. frankenstein

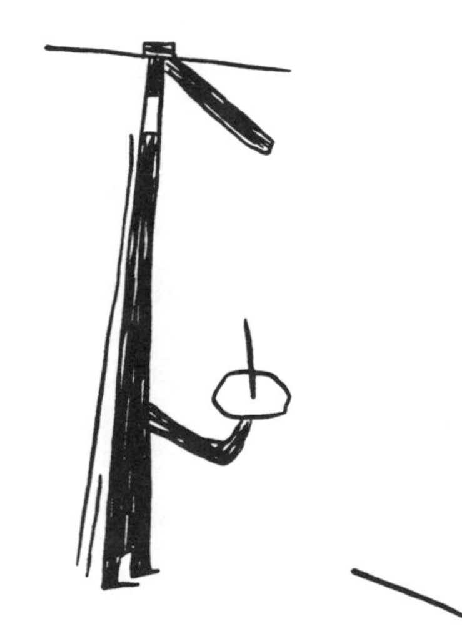

MAHLER

van helsing's night off

MAHLER

Mahler lives and works in Vienna, Austria.
Most of his comic-books have been published by L`ASSOCIATION, Paris.
He also writes and illustrates picture-books for children and adults. His strip "Flaschko - The Man in the Electric Blanket" has been turned into a series of short animated films, and has shown at numerous festivals around the world. website: www.mahlermuseum.at

major works:
Lone Racer (L´Association, Paris 1999)
TNT (L`Association, Paris 1999)
Lame Ryder (L´Association, Paris 2001)
*Emanuelle`s Last Flight* (L`Association, Paris 2001)
Désir (éditions de la pastèque, Montreal 2001)
Kratochvil (L´Association, Paris 2002)
Flaschko (L`Association, Paris 2003)
Les Souffrances du Jeune Frankenstein (L`Ampoule, Paris 2003)

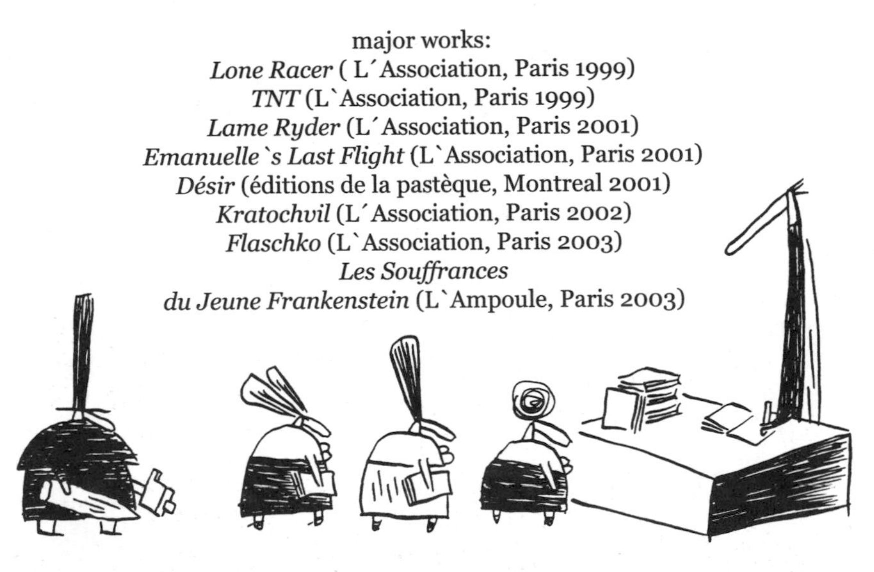